Lessons From the Wilderness

Barbara Huddleston-Mattai

Lessons From the Wilderness

© 2006 by Barbara Huddleston-Mattai

ISBN 978-1-4357-0016-1

Published by BARBARA HUDDLESTON-MATTAI, 204 Portside Buffalo, New York 14202

All rights reserved. No portion of this book may be reproduced, stored in a retrieval system, or transmitted in any form or by any means, electronic, mechanical, recording or otherwise, without prior written permission of the author.

All scripture quotations and references are taken from the *New King James Version* (NKJV). Copyright © 1979, 1980, 1982 by Thomas Nelson, Inc. Used by permission. All rights reserved.

Printed in the United States of America.

Lulu.com

Preface

Lessons From the Wilderness is about the trials and challenges everyone encounters in a lifetime. It uses the wilderness journeys of the Israelites, beginning with Abraham, as well as contemporary situations, and demonstrates what is to be learned from the symbolic wildernesses of our lives. One person's "wilderness" may be that time of devastating illness. For another, the loss of a loved one may shift her/him into a wilderness experience. Basically, it represents those periods when one feels alone, discomforted, and without recourse. However, the wilderness offers opportunities wherein much can be learned. For example, the children of Israel's failure to initially enter the Promised land teaches us that God is to be believed above everything else, including the opinions and reports of others as well as the challenges of the circumstances. Also, each wilderness has a purpose. It comes to help get us to the place we are destined to go. Learning how to go through the experience and reap what is to be gained from it can cause us to grow spiritually and can prepare us for that place. Grasping the significance of the journey may help us progress through it without undue stress and worry, and can help us rest while in the situation. The wilderness therefore may be embraced with courage, confidence and anticipation. It is even possible to experience joy during the process as we look forward to the rewards that will accompany the departure from it, a departure that will surely come.

Lessons From the Wilderness is designed so that you might place yourself and your circumstances in the wilderness experiences of each chapter. As you read, allow the conditions and lessons to speak to your situation. You are also encouraged to read the accompanying scripture references. This book will provide instructions for proceeding through and emerging from these experiences triumphantly.

At any one time, we are either in a trial, coming out of one or on our way into one. These are the wildernesses of life.

"Behold I will do a new thing,

Now it shall spring forth;

Shall you not know it?

I will even make a road in the wilderness

And rivers in the desert" (Isaiah 43:19).

Contents

Preface		3
Introduction		9
I.	Entry Into the Wilderness	13
II.	A Place of Testing	19
III.	Viewing the Promise	27
IV.	Learning to Sacrifice, Intercede, Feast, Praise & Worship	35
V.	A Place of Isolation	45
VI.	A Place of Deception	50
VII.	A Place of Discernment	57
VIII.	Discovering Jehovah/Yahew	65
IX.	Learning to Reverence God	76

X.	Learning to Overcome your Enemies	85
XI.	Learning the Consequence of Unrepentant Sin	95
XII.	Learning to Die	100
XIII.	Learning to Listen	110
XIV.	Learning to Love	119
XV.	Learning to Build (The Temple)	128
XVI.	Learning to Possess the Land	135
XVII.	Remembering the Victory & Standing in the Triumph	145
XVIII.	Conclusion	153
References		177

Introduction

Webster's Collegiate Dictionary (1983) defines "wilderness" as "a tract or region uncultivated (not prepared or used for raising crops, i.e. nothing life sustaining or of profit grows there; the soil has not been broken or loosened so that crops may grow) and is uninhabited by humans." It is a place where nothing needful or of value seems to grow because conditions there are not suited for most life forms or for vital maturation. *Vine's Expository Dictionary* (1997) defines "wilderness" as a "desolate (uninhabited, joyless, disconsolate, sorrowful, gloomy) deserted, lonely place." These definitions bring to mind a picture of a barren and sparse land, which is true to some degree, but a wilderness can also include grassy plains as well as plant life and water sources [places of refreshing and rest (Youngblood, 1995)]. Therefore, the wilderness can also be a source of life, nourishment and provision. Although it may initially appear not to have the things necessary for abundant life, a closer look shows that helpful and needful things do indeed grow there, things which can sustain life and help in the growth process.

In a symbolic way, a wilderness can be viewed as that time when and place where we are at a standstill, a point from which we seem to be unable to move. It is where we find ourselves feeling isolated and alone, where it is difficult for us to be comforted, and the place where we feel God has deserted us because it seems He no longer hears our prayers. It is that place where we feel our sorrow and trouble are so deep there is no relief, at least in the near future. In this place our faith appears to be absent or it is so small it might as well be considered as such. In this place, we may feel our very "life" is at stake.

However, the "wilderness" can also include times of refreshing and feelings of relief, dependent upon our finding and making use of the resources there. If we truly search for these resources and use them for our survival, the wilderness becomes a place which is ripe for us to come to an end of ourselves as we have known ourselves to be, a place where we find what is needed to grow and develop into a better self. In the final analysis, when the wilderness journey is completed, it is the place from which we will come forth with at least some loss of our solid footing, never to be regained, or with a more solid foundation and greater faith in our Creator. Some of our greatest "wilderness" lessons can be learned from the Israelites who provide examples of both outcomes. We can learn from their experiences as we travel through the symbolic wildernesses of our

lives.

I.

Entry Into the Wilderness

Hagar was pregnant with the child of her mistress Sarai's husband, Abram. It was not of Hagar's design; her mistress wanted children, she could not have them, and acting on a custom of the time, Sarai gave Hagar to Abram for a procreative union so that she might have a child through her maid. Now that Hagar was pregnant, perhaps due to pride, she despised Sarai. Sarai retaliated by treating her so harshly that Hagar ran away into the wilderness (Genesis 16:1-7).

Entry into the wilderness can be the result of several circumstances. As with Hagar, sometimes conditions over which we have little control can drive us into a deserted place. At other times, we choose the wilderness to flee from situations that we think will have no positive outcome; that is, we believe them to be hopeless. Elijah running from Jezebel is one such example (1st Kings 19:2-3). In both situations, the outcome is usually the result of relying on ourselves, when we have forgotten Who is really in charge of our course of events.

Then at other times, we are led into a wilderness. Joseph found himself there because of the jealousy of his brothers (Genesis 37:5-10, 18-24), and Jesus was led there by the Holy Spirit (Mark 1:12). In both cases, a purpose was to be served and preparation was to occur through the wilderness experience.

The way by which we arrive in the wilderness is important because it can set the tone for what will be accomplished there. As with Hagar and Elijah, we may take ourselves to this place before we are ready to endure the challenges which are common in that territory. When we take ourselves there, we may find that we are in a place of discomfort, a place for which we are not quite ready, for which we have not been prepared and are not yet "fit" for this type of training, and for which we do not have the strength for the period of time we must remain there. A divinely orchestrated wilderness, however, comes at a time when we are most ready to receive its training, when we are most ready to learn what it must teach us. Only our Father knows when we are prepared, even if it is unknown to us, to learn its lessons. He knows exactly how to tailor the experience, how long it will take to learn the lessons, and exactly what is to be accomplished in the process. He structures the entire affair so that the greatest results are accomplished in the most suitable period of time and process. Going there before it is time may result in having to return to the previous situation until we are prepared to receive what the wilderness offers. Hagar was told by God: "Return to your mistress, and submit yourself under her hand" (Genesis 16:9). On his way to the wilderness Elijah was told to return and get back to the job to which he was called, that of being a prophet (1 Kings 19:5-16). Proceeding to the wilderness on our own may result in the undue stress and frustration that comes from delaying our progress and from having to return to already covered ground.

Being led into the wilderness assures us that there is no mistake. Genesis 37 demonstrates that the jealousy of his brothers resulted in Joseph being thrown into a pit in the wilderness; however, the experience served the purposes of God. Joseph had to be prepared to take his place as second only to Pharaoh. Maturation and discernment had to develop. He had to learn how to be in charge. He had to learn how to be exalted while remaining humble, and he could only accomplish that, first, by being humbled. We can know that God was controlling the event because no water was in the pit at the time Joseph was placed there (vs. 24). If water had been present, he could have at the least been in physical danger, and at the most, killed. If God has led us there, it is certain He will not allow us to be destroyed by our wildernesses. As it was with Joseph, so it is with us. Whatever we go through during that time is all part of the process, the road that leads to our destiny. They are the things we need to get us ready for our God given purpose. It is the wilderness that prepares us for our ministry. It is that place which serves several purposes, and just as with Hagar, regardless of how we arrived and the circumstances which brought us there, it is there that we will learn God as El Roi, the God who sees us, no matter where we are.

II.

A Place of Testing

Sarah, Hagar's mistress, conceived and bore a child in her old age, something no one expected or thought possible. Once Isaac (Sarah's baby) was born, Sarah had no use for Hagar. Perhaps Sarah was prideful. Maybe she was resentful, or maybe she was a little of both. Whatever the cause, she did not want Hagar or her son around as a reminder of the joint inheritance her son would share with Isaac, nor perhaps did she want him there to compete with Isaac in any form. Now Hagar and her son must go. Sarah told Abraham to send them away (Genesis 21:1-14). Upon the counsel of God, he sent the two away with bread and water. They wandered into the wilderness. After a time, they had no more water, and Hagar perceived that both she and her son would die (vs. 15-16).

Have you ever been in that place? Have you ever found yourself in a situation due to circumstances beyond your control where you felt alone and in dire despair, where the road has come to a dead end and there is no place for you to go? A place where all you could do was cry out to the Lord and even then you feared nothing was going to happen? That is the place of Hagar. These are certainly conditions which can try the foundations of our faith, the point where the core of our belief system is tested.

The children of Israel also found themselves in a similar situation. After they had crossed the Red Sea, they went into the wilderness of Shur (Exodus 15:22-

24). The scripture tells us that they found no water. They went farther to a place called Marah and could not drink the water there because it was bitter. The things they had learned about God were under trial. Were His provisions unlimited? How many times could they call and He would answer? The real question was would their faith withstand the testing these circumstances were presenting. We are informed that their response was to complain against Moses and the situation. He cried out to the Lord and as a result was instructed what to do to acquire water for them.

What do you do when you are in your deserted place and the resources dry up? Do you grumble and complain or do you cry out to the Lord? Do you confidently wait to hear the Lord answer because you are expecting Him to respond, or do you doubt and give in to despair?

Wilderness soil is fertile for doubt and fear. It is the place where the enemy of God's people seizes the opportunity to bring thoughts of God as being untrustworthy, thoughts that He will allow us at the least to be damaged, and at the most, destroyed. This enemy tells us God is not going to answer, that He has deserted us and, therefore, we are left to our own devices. These are untruths and therefore unproductive thoughts to entertain. Scripture tells us we must cast down these arguments and ideas that exalt (are raised in rank and power) themselves against the knowledge of God (what we know about Him) and that we must bring every thought into captivity to the obedience of Christ (2nd Corinthians 10:5), meaning that we must throw off, get rid of any thoughts or ideas that do not line up with God's word and our knowledge of Him. We must take control of our thoughts, making sure that what we think agrees with what Christ has said, that our reasoning is based on His word and His works.

Anything which goes against the word of God must be discarded and replaced with His word. In the wilderness, Satan presented propositions to Christ (Matthew 4:1-11). Implied in his temptations was the call for Christ to either show Himself prematurely (before the crucifixion) or the challenge to prove Himself through ways dictated by Satan and therefore not ordained by God. Yielding to any of these proposals would have been outside the will of God and would have bypassed the purposes and plan of God. Our salvation would have been compromised. Jesus replied with God's word. Because He passed the tests, we have the comfort of knowing that, although He was tempted, He did not yield to the temptation, and we are given the same ability to not yield to the temptations we face.

Satan will do the same to us. He will try to convince us to go around God's plan or to dishonor the name of Christ. In our wilderness, he will tempt us with things which appeal to our carnal desires, anything he believes will pull us away from God and His plan for us. For example, we may be lured into remaining in bed in order to sleep longer when we have set our minds and determined to get up early to pray. Or he may entice us to food during the time we have dedicated to fasting. It is no accident that one of your favorite foods, through no effort of your own, will be made available to you during this time. Or ultimately he will try to deceive us into thinking the outcome of the wilderness is not worth the process, the cost for what we desire is too much. Surrendering to these arguments and ideas can cause us to feel we are on our own, that what happens depends on us. When our thinking is centered on our strength, we tend to go ahead of God and travel onto a path which may lead us away from the very thing which is needed to move us forward in Christ. These may be the exact conditions necessary for us to mature in Him, to be promoted to a new level in Him. This may be the very place wherein your prayer will be answered, the prayer you prayed to be more like Christ. Did He not also go through a wilderness experience before He moved into His purpose? It is from the crucible of fire that pure gold comes forth, gold that can be used for beautiful and elaborate works and other instruments of value. Like Jesus, you must fight back with the Word of God. You must not allow the enemy to rob you of the benefits that will come from this experience. You must know "we have become partakers of Christ if we hold the beginning of our confidence steadfast to the end" (Hebrews 3:14). We must increase our faith by realizing that God causes all things to work together for our good (Romans 8:28). He will never allow anything to happen to us which is not absolutely necessary for character development. Your wilderness has been allowed by Him for your growth.

It will be our loss if we submit to the enticements of Satan. If we surrender, we will have failed the test of our faith in God, and the reward that comes from continuing to be steadfast will have been compromised or lost. We cannot afford to lose sight of the promise.

III.

Viewing the Promise

Hagar positioned herself and her son to die (Genesis 21:14-16). After her resources, bread and water, were consumed, doubt and fear crept in. She doubted there was any possible way they could survive, and she feared seeing her child die.

Cassandra had a son who was the result of much praying, prophesying and faith. For many years she had been barren. She vowed as Hannah had done (1 Samuel 1:11) that if the Lord would bless her with a child, she would be diligent in giving that child back to Him. He heard and granted her request. As the child grew in her womb, Cassandra meditated upon the vow she had made. One of the prophecies foretold that this child would be a mighty warrior in the Lord's service. But as the son matured into young adulthood, she witnessed his move in directions away from God and toward the things of the world. Doubt and fear entered her spirit and she wondered what might become of the promised son.

All of us have been in this place at one time or another. We know what God has spoken to us, but the circumstances seem to indicate something different. Doubt and fear arise. Someone in Cassandra's position might ask: "Did I really hear from God or did these thoughts originate in my own mind? Maybe I misread Him and only heard what I wanted to hear. Perhaps the prophet(ess) and consequently the prophecy were not on target. Maybe God has changed His mind. Even more, I am afraid of what God might do to get this child to the place He desires him to be. What if He allows him, like the prodigal son, to go to the pigpen to bring him to himself, or to the pit to humble him? Who can know the mind of God?"

It is at this point that a decision must be made: Which report will we believe? What vision will we grasp? When Moses sent men to spy out the Promised Land of Canaan, they reported the land as being all God said it was (Numbers 13:27-33; 14). The land did indeed flow with milk and honey, and it brought forth fruit abundantly. However, some of the spies saw it as a fortified city filled with giants and men who were stronger than they, a land they would not be able to conquer. But two men of the group had a vision of their God as being stronger than any man or giant who might come upon them, and viewed Him as well able to give the children of Israel possession of the land as He had promised.

Which vision do you hold on to when you come to a fork in the road and a decision must be made about whether to proceed or retreat? Will you allow giants to stop you? Will you be unable to take possession of the promise because, although you have seen the Lord's glory, the signs which He performed, and have put Him to the test, you still do not have the faith to heed His voice (Numbers 14:22-23), to believe what He said? Have you, like the children of Israel, forgotten His previous works (Deuteronomy 1:30)? Do you not remember how He parted the "waters" of your adversity so that you might cross into the position everyone said you would not be able to assume? Or do you not recall how God dealt with your enemies to the extent that they are no longer present in your life? Has He ever once failed to deliver what He promised? Will your promise die with you in the wilderness because you complain against God in unbelief (Numbers 14:29)? Will your children reap the consequences of your disbelief (Numbers 14:31-33)? Will they also have to endure hardships you have created because of your doubting when they could have been enjoying the fruit of the promised possession?

We learn from Hagar that in our isolated, lonely, uncertain places, we must remember the promises of God; it is critical to our survival. He had promised her that Ishmael would grow up and live in the presence of his brethren (Genesis 16:12). How would he live in the presence of his brethren if he had died while still in his youth in isolation with his mother? Similarly, the Lord had given Cassandra a promise. How could her son be a mighty warrior for the Lord if he would be given over to the world? We have the tendency when the situation becomes critical to abandon the promises and to focus on and cling to the threat, just as Hagar did. Keeping our focus on God's assurance and on His guarantees of deliverance will destroy the perceived threats of our present condition.

God promised the children of Israel the land of Canaan. Would He not give them the power needed to possess what He had promised? Would His promise fall short because they believed they did not have the resources needed to bring it to pass? Is He not able of Himself to bring forth what He has promised? He has said without Him, you can do nothing (John 15:5); therefore, we know we do not have the ability to bring the promises to pass on our own. We also know He is more than able to bring them forth, and we can rely on Him to do so. "Has He said, and will He not do? Or has

He spoken, and will He not make it good" (Numbers 23:19)?

When faith is waning and hope has diminished, Habakkuk 2:3 instructs us that "the vision is yet for an appointed time; but at the end it will speak, and it will not lie. Though it tarries, wait for it because it will surely come; it will not tarry." We must remember God cannot lie and what He has purposed **will** come to pass. It is the enemy's job to have us believe what God has spoken is not true, just as he deceived Eve (Genesis 3:1-4). It is his job to delude us into thinking that what God said is not really the way He meant it, not the way it will turn out. In doing his job, he attempts to make us believe the Lord plays games with us to trick us, just to see what we will do, certainly not for the purpose of our growth and maturity. It is to our benefit to call forth all we know about God, all we have experienced about

Him, and all He has told us about Himself in His word. It is on these things that we meditate and take our stand. "Therefore do not cast away your confidence, which has great reward. For you have need of endurance, so that after you have done the will of God, you may receive the promise: For yet a little while, And He who is coming will come and will not tarry" (Hebrews 10:35-37). However, the will of God and hence receiving the promise may require a sacrifice, a living sacrifice.

IV.

Learning to Sacrifice, Intercede, Feast, Praise, and Worship

During the time the children of Israel were in captivity in Egypt, the elders were told by Moses and Aaron that God had seen their affliction, heard their cry, and knew their sorrows. Pharaoh was told that God wanted the Israelites freed so that they might hold "a feast" to Him (Exodus 5:1), and that they might worship Him in the wilderness (Exodus 7:16). A plea was made for Pharaoh to allow the children of Israel to "go three days' journey into the wilderness and sacrifice to the Lord our God as He will command us" (Exodus 8:27).

After some time Pharaoh not only agreed, but further asked Moses to intercede for him (vs. 28).

Arthur is what many would call a "go-getter." He works long hours, and when he is not working, he is thinking of work. He would like to spend more time with God, but something urgent always seems to get in the way; there's always something that needs to be done in order to keep his head above water. One day Arthur begins to have pain over his entire body; he aches day and night. The doctor tells him he has a serious viral infection, and if it is not taken care of, could cause him serious, permanent damage. He has to be on complete bed rest for at least a month. He has no other choice but to comply. How will he handle this period of sacrifice; what will he do? What will be the outcome for him of this time? What will be the nature of his relationship with the Lord during and after this period?

Being in slavery, the children of Israel most likely spent the majority of their time following the orders of their tasks masters from sunup to sundown. There may have been little time for worship and not much thought of praise. Feasting with the Lord would compete with the chores of day-to-day living, and intercession probably had little chance of getting beyond praying for the conditions of one's own circumstances. Even if the Israelites did sacrifice, intercede, feast, worship, and praise, there was good likelihood it may have been to false gods, for they had learned the ways of the Egyptians. In Amos 5:26, they are condemned: "You also carried along Sikkuth your king and Chiun, your idols, the star of your gods, which you made for yourselves." Because of this, they would have to get to know the only true and living God and would have to learn to serve Him solely. A sojourn in the wilderness would be the beginning of accomplishing that goal.

Sometimes we also can become so busy in day-to-day affairs that we fail to spend the concentrated time needed to fellowship with the Lord, the time needed to be in that intimate place with Him wherein He is worshipped, praised, and honored. It is to the place of intimacy we bring Him our sacrifices, feast with Him, and present our requests to Him, not just our own, but others' also. It is a place of sweet communion. Many times we have questions and petitions before the Lord, but we expect him to answer while we are involved in non-stop busyness. Perhaps He has answered, but we have failed to slow down long enough to listen. Or our answers may have been delayed because we have not given Him the respect of our undivided attention, that focused time. It cannot be said that God will not answer during your busy times, but Lamentations (3:25-26) informs us that the Lord will reward those who seek Him and wait quietly for the move of His hand. Even Jesus isolated Himself so that He could commune with the Father in this manner (Matthew 14:23; Luke 9:18).

The wilderness is one of the most advantageous places and provides a great opportunity for offerings, showing reverence, and fellowshipping with the Lord. Because it is a "desolate" place, there can be fewer distractions. It becomes a place where one can draw closer to God, and this worship will always be rewarded with intimacy. To worship means to revere, to regard as worthy of profound honor and respect, and to have deeper feelings of tenderness (Merriam-Webster, 1983). How can this be achieved except through focused time spent alone with the One revered. "Draw near to God and He will draw near to you" (James 4:8). Who can be closer to God than the one who realizes s/he is alone except for the knowledge of His presence? Although we may not feel Him, the realization of His presence alone may cause us to cling to Him because we know He is the only One Who can aid us while we are here, and the only One Who can bring us out of the wilderness.

Satan does not want you to enter this place of intimacy because he knows the "effective, fervent prayer of a righteous man avails much" (James 5:16). This is the time when he will try to distract you with unrelated thoughts, the telephone ringing, someone wanting something only "you" can provide, or an "emergency" which "demands" your attention. But you must be determined in your pursuit of God. Luke (18:2-6) reminds us of the woman who persisted before the judge who had no regard for God or man. Because she persevered in her request, it was granted "lest by her continual coming she weary" him. The scripture further informs that if an unjust judge would grant a persistent request, God will hear us when we call to Him (Psalm 4:3).

The wilderness can provide the conditions and motivation to move closer to God and, consequently, experience Him in new ways, to see Him work in ways not previously witnessed.

Moses' initial request of Pharaoh on behalf of the children of Israel indicates that the wilderness is also a place for sacrifice (Exodus 8:27-28). Where is this place in our wilderness? It is where we offer God something which costs us. It may be the sin we have consistently committed. It may be our pride, our rights, our children, our spouse, our finances, or our occupation, those things we have tried to control. It is the place in the wilderness where we put them on the altar, relinquish them to God, and place them under His control. The cost will be to not yield to the yearnings of our carnal nature which wants to hold on to these things, to satisfy itself, to protect itself, and to be in control. When we try to control things ourselves, we are in essence saying we do not trust God. Most often, what we are really saying is we do not trust Him to perform it in the manner we desire; that desire is usually for God to do what He will, but do it without much discomfort. However, change by its very nature implies some degree of discomfort. And, there can be no growth without change. In this area of the wilderness, maturity can develop.

When Pharaoh gave his consent to the wilderness request, he asked Moses to pray for him. The wilderness then can also be a place of intercession. However, at this time, to intercede might be a sacrifice. Praise and worship may be also. "How can I intercede for someone else, praise God, and worship Him when **I'm** under such trying circumstances, when I am in such a desolate place?" Yet sometimes, as we pray for others, we are released from our anxiety and care. We find that as we "lose our lives" on behalf of someone else, it is then that we truly find it: in service to others. As we find our true lives, we find our hearts filled with praise and this praise will lead us into worship of the One who truly gives life. We are told to "rejoice **always** (emphasis added), pray without ceasing, in everything give thanks; for this is the will of God in Christ Jesus for you" (1st Thessalonians 5:16). We can do this as we reaffirm that fervent prayer yields results and as we rejoice in the hope (confident expectation, according to *Vine's Dictionary*) that God is going to do what He promised. Thanks are given because we also know we have what we have asked of Him, as long as it is according to His will.

V.

A Place of Isolation

As Jacob waited alone in the wilderness to meet Esau, he surely pondered what his fate would be upon their encounter. He had sent his household ahead, and there he was left with only his thoughts (Genesis 32:22-32). During the night he wrestled with a Man until the break of day. Jacob prevailed and was blessed.

Tabitha's husband's funeral was yesterday. He was not only her provider, but he was also her best friend. For a week, the house had been filled with people who came to comfort her and pay their last respects. Now, they had all gone, and she was left alone. What will she do? How will she take care of herself? Who will be there for her when she is lonely?

All of us can identify with either or both of these situations. We have found ourselves in the wilderness of isolation. Usually, our first response is to do something, anything to remove ourselves from this place. Although this is not where we want to be, we must remember that this place of aloneness is no mistake, and it is not by chance. Nothing can happen to us unless it passes by God first (Job 9-12); therefore, He has surely allowed it. Because we know everything God does has a purpose, there is a purpose to be accomplished in this situation also, and if you will struggle with your challenge until your dawn breaks (you begin to see relief), you will be blessed.

Sometimes, it is in isolation that we begin to closely examine ourselves and our situation. When we are alone, pretenses can be abandoned. We are then in a position to confront those things which have been hidden from our view or we have refused to see. Those sins which "so easily beset" us can be faced by first acknowledging them, repenting (turning away from) by taking them to the Lord, and finally allowing Him to cleanse us of them. In the wilderness, because we are alone, we may not be hindered by the opinions of others who might have a tendency to minimize our sins or to make excuses for them. In this place where there is only you and God, honesty can be total and complete. There is no need to put up a façade because God already knows all there is to know about you, even more than you know about yourself. He knew these things before they ever entered your mind; therefore, He cannot be fooled. Realizing this truth is liberating, allowing us the opportunity to come before Him in all sincerity and honesty. It is the place where upon leaving, sin is left behind and the need for pretenses will no longer exist. Herein lays true freedom.

It is also during the lonely and isolated times that we realize our need for and total dependence on God. It was in the isolated place that the Lord came to bless Jacob, and it can also be in your lonely place that you receive a blessing. It is here Tabitha can begin to realize it was really God all along taking care of her through her husband. God warned the children of Israel against thinking that their power and might had gained them wealth (Deuteronomy 8:17-18). He reminded them that it was He Who gave them their power to get wealth. We are also reminded that "love is of God; and everyone who loves is born of God and knows God" (1st John

4:7). Therefore, all the things that her husband was able to do and demonstrate originated with and proceeded from God. In this place of aloneness, Tabitha can learn she has access to the same God Who moved through her husband. He can provide **all** of her needs.

Jacob told the Lord he would not let Him go until He blessed him (Genesis 32:25-26, 32). You may have to "wrestle" with your situation "until the break of day," but just as it was with Jacob, in the process you may be changed forever. Your change will be a reminder of the greatness of God and His ability to do what He wills. The blessing will be worth so much more than the toil, and it has repercussions that last for eternity. "Weeping may endure for a night, but joy comes in the morning" (Psalm 30:5).

VI.

A Place of Deception

The children of Israel had been defeated at Ai (Joshua 7:5). Then the Lord spoke to Joshua and told him He had delivered the King of Ai, his people, his city, and his land into Joshua's hand (Joshua 8:1). Having received this knowledge, Joshua developed a battle plan which included pretending to be defeated so that the city could be ambushed and seized from the rear. Israel killed all the inhabitants of Ai and took the spoils of the city as booty for themselves. This very appearance of defeat proved to be the conquering of the enemy.

Jessica, after struggling through years of abuse, and praying to and believing God for deliverance, had now been deserted by her husband, the result of an affair with another woman. She felt defeated, as if God had failed her. Why had He not answered her prayers? Why had He not "fixed" her marriage? Jessica did not realize that this appearance of defeat was actually the long sought answer to her many prayers.

Oftentimes we retreat to the wilderness as a perceived haven because we feel we have been defeated or have failed at something we pursued. Our view of the situation only extends as far as the consequences of this loss. Thoughts of the outcome and how we arrived there fill our minds. Feelings of despair and finality consume us. In these places of perceived defeat, it is so important to realize that the battle is not over until the victory is ours. 2nd Corinthians 2:14 tell us that we **always** triumph in Christ. Therein lies the true power, in Christ Who can never fail. The apostle Paul adds to our instruction by letting us know the Lord's strength is made perfect in our weaknesses. Our infirmities make it necessary for the power of Christ to rest on us (2nd Corinthians 12:9) so that we are able to do what must be done. We can **never** be defeated because Christ is with us, His Spirit resides in us. To think otherwise is to be deceived. When Jesus and the disciples were on a boat, a great windstorm arose (Mark 4:35-40). The disciples were afraid and, therefore, awoke Jesus who was asleep in the stern. They asked if He did not care that they were perishing. Jesus, through His rebuke of the wind and command to the sea, calmed the storm. He then rebuked the disciples for having no faith. A review of the account calls for us to ask how they could have possibly perished with Jesus on the boat. How could the

Master of both wind and water have been destroyed by the very elements over which He has control? They had not fully realized His purpose or His power. We have that same Jesus with us.

The stillness and isolation of the wilderness enhances your ability to realistically review your situation. The atmosphere of this place will seem to compel you to meditate on your predicament. During this time you must ask: "How can I possibly fail when there is no failure in Christ, when He is with me and in me?" If you have acknowledged Him in all things and allowed Him to direct your path, you cannot fail. Even if you have not previously done this, every moment provides an opportunity to begin. You are in a prime position to turn things around. Perhaps that is why you have arrived here.

Sometimes, what appears to be failure is just God's way of providing what we need and of preparing us to fulfill the purpose and plan that He surely has for our lives. Joshua's seeming defeat led to conquering the land as well as booty for him and all of Israel. It also increased his faith for future battles. Jessica failed to see that she had indeed been delivered from that abusive situation and was now in a position for God to bless her in a way she had never imagined. Many times, because God does not move in the way we expect or the way we desire, we believe that our prayers have not been heard or answered. But God's ways are not our ways. We see for only a short distance, and He sees from everlasting-to-everlasting, for eternity. He knows our destination and the good things He has in store for us. He also knows how to get us to that end while providing the things we need and ridding us of the things which will be hindrances. Only He knows what is truly the very best. Often, we are asking Him for one thing and He has something greater in mind. Have you ever asked God for something you really wanted, something you just knew would be great for you and He allowed you to have it only for you to later regret having ever received it? If we submit our wills to His, He will give us only what is absolutely the best, and only that which fits into His plan for our lives. If only we could see as God sees, we would want nothing more or less than what He gives because we would realize He knows what is needed and what will reap the greatest good in our lives. We desire the best; He desires to give us the perfect.

When Elijah felt defeated by Jezebel, he wanted to die (1st Kings 19:1-4). God had to reveal to him that indeed he would not die, but rather he had a job to do: he must anoint two kings and a prophet (vs. 15-16). Not only did Elijah not know he would not see death, but he also did not know he would be taken to heaven in a chariot sent by God Himself! Who knows what awaits you after this brief interlude with deception? One thing is certain, if you remain focused on Christ, you will come out of this period with new knowledge of Him and more faith in what He is able to do. Hold on. You are not defeated! It only appears to be so; it is surely a deception. The result, your victory, will prove to be well worth the wait.

VII.

A Place of Discernment

As Moses and the children of Israel were traveling in the wilderness, God told Moses not to "meddle" with the descendents of Esau (Deuteronomy 2:4-5). He was told not to "harass" or "contend" with these Moabites in battle. However, the Lord also said He had given into his hand Sihon the Amorite, king of Heshbon, and his land (vs. 24). Moses' testimony was they did not go anywhere God had forbidden them (vs. 37).

Alexandra's husband spent time with his buddies whenever he wanted, watched what he wanted on television, and listened to whatever he wanted on the radio. He complained, however, whenever Alexandra went to church or wanted to watch or listen to Christian programs. This produced constant tension in their home. She didn't know quite what to do. During those times when she objected, strong arguments ensued. Now she was not sure if she should continue to voice her feelings or just hold her peace.

In both the above cases, the will of God must be known so that He can be obeyed. Both situations require discernment of God's voice and His ways. However, this discernment will bring with it the responsibility of obedience. Pursuing a path of disobedience and one He has not sanctioned invite confusion and discord.

Vine's Dictionary (1997) defines discernment as distinguishing, separating, investigating, examining, and scrutinizing." Because you are alone, the wilderness is a prime location to truly learn to distinguish God's voice. By investigating, examining, and scrutinizing all voices, you may learn to separate His from that of another. Your motivation will come from the realization that your very survival depends on knowing His voice and following His guidance. Only He can successfully lead you from this place. Therein lays a most wonderful opportunity to learn to separate your thoughts from those that originate with Him. It is also the opportune time to investigate, examine, and study your motives and the condition of your heart. How did you really get here? What did you do that added to your arrival on this path? What part did you play?

It is here that you may also learn God's purpose and plan for your life and in what ways you have followed His path or how you have drifted from it. Knowing and adhering to His will for you will direct your choices. Necessary to this process is learning, studying, and meditating on God's word. His word is the rod and standard by which you will measure your character and behavior. He is the image with which you are to compare yourself. How will you truly know the standards and how will you know His will if you do not know His word? One litmus test of God's voice is that it will **never** contradict His word; His will agrees with His word. Therefore, you must know His word.

This is also the place where you may learn which battles to fight and where you may ultimately learn that none of the battles are yours, but rather they are the Lord's. God told Moses He would put dread and fear of the children of Israel upon the nations and because of that report, those nations would tremble and be in anguish of them (Deuteronomy 2:25). It would not be necessary for them to fight all the wars. Deuteronomy

2:30 instructs us that God is able to deliver our enemies into our hands if He so chooses. He told Joshua that He, Himself, was the One fighting for him (3:22). It is the Lord Who sets the stage for the outcome of the battles, if you submit to Him. In learning this lesson, you will find that you can rest in Him. You can trust Him to instruct you concerning what you are to do, if anything, in which battles, and you can also trust Him for the outcome.

In the wilderness, God told Moses whom to fight and whom to leave alone. He told him who had been delivered into his hand and who had not. In Alexandra's wilderness, God will also tell her when to speak and when to keep quiet. He will let her know which battle He has delivered into her hands and the ones with which she should not "meddle." Just as Moses had, Alexandra must also have a discerning ear, must know the voice of

God, must have spent time with God, and she must learn obedience. The wilderness creates an atmosphere that is optimal for all four.

The word of God teaches His will. Once you know His will, you will know for what and whom to pray. Sometimes we pray "amiss" because we are praying contrary to God's will; we have not discerned it. I John (5:14) tells us that we can have confidence and know our requests are granted if we ask according to the will of God. Some of us have witnessed prayers being offered for the healing of one who is sick. The person was not healed, but rather died. It was God's will to bring him/her to Himself. If there had been discernment on the part of those who were praying, the requests of the prayers might have been different. For example, there might rather have been petitions for strength, for comfort, for ease of suffering, for a peaceful journey home, and for eternal healing.

Sometimes we know the will of God, yet ask Him to grant the desires of our heart, which may not be in agreement with His will. Oftentimes He will grant it. We should remember, however, that God knows what is best, and His **perfect** will is always unsurpassed. How many times have we asked something of God and, in His **permissive** will, He has granted it, only later for us to bemoan the trouble that thing has brought us? It is best to go with God's way. Jesus, as always, provided the perfect example. In His prayer in the Garden of Gethsemane, He asked to have the "cup" removed. However, He went on to acknowledge His willingness to submit to the will of God. That is an example well worth following, especially for those whose trust is in Him. Pray for discernment concerning the heart of God, obey His directives, and trust Him for the outcome. He is Jehovah God.

VIII.

Discovering Jehovah/Yahew

When Moses and Aaron first went to see Pharaoh to request that the children of Israel be allowed a three day's journey into the wilderness to offer sacrifices to God, Pharaoh's response was to increase the Israelites' work tasks (Exodus 5:1-20). Also, the officers placed in charge of them were beaten and pressured to meet the work quota. Confused about Pharaoh's actions, the people questioned him about his treatment of them. Having been told that it was due to Moses' and Aaron's request, the officers then blamed and pronounced a curse on them. Moses went back to the Lord and asked about His original promise to deliver the Israelites (vs. 22-23). God said to Moses, "I appeared to Abraham, to Isaac, and to Jacob, as God Almighty, but by My name Lord I was not known to them" (Exodus 6:3). "Therefore say to the children of Israel: I am the Lord; . . ." (vs. 6).

Johnna and her husband have spent their wealth unwisely. Now they are in financial distress. Bills are due, and bill collectors are calling. They have acknowledged their sins before the Lord and have continued to tithe and give offerings in spite of their circumstances. They do not know what to do. Needing a financial blessing, they have no resource other than the Lord.

The name YHWH, pronounced Yahweh in Hebrew and Jehovah as the English equivalent, means "He Is," "I Am Who I Am," or "I Am Who I will be"

(Youngblood, 1995). These definitions are meant to capture the essence of Who God is, which means He is Whatever and Whomever He determines Himself to be. There is nothing He cannot do. He always has been and always will be; He is eternal. All things were made by Him and all things belong to Him. He knows all things, and He is in all places at all times. Some of us have known God in a theoretical sense, but we have not experienced Him in these ways. It was in the wilderness that the children of Israel became acquainted with His character. The wilderness provided the distressing circumstances whereby their needs became evident and there was no resource other than God. In those truly isolated places, we learn the awesome power and the provisions of God. In other environments we might call someone we know or ask someone who we believe can help. We might also depend on our resources or the resources of another source. We might call in a favor owed, or appeal to someone's guilt or other emotion to move her/him to help us. But none of these will work in the wilderness because we believe we are alone. The children of Israel learned that their most basic needs could not be met outside of God's hand. There was no one else. They only had each other, and all of them were in the same situation. God had arranged it that way. Although they plundered Egypt before they left, they had not been able to carry enough water and food for the entire journey. They would have to depend on Him.

God showed the Israelites that He was able to be all they needed Him to be (El Shaddai- All-sufficient God). When the water was undrinkable and when there was no water in the wilderness, He provided it for them [Jehovah-Jireh – The Lord will provide (Exodus 15:22-

25; 17:1-6)]. When they were hungry, He provided food (16:2-12). In all their wilderness wanderings, we are told the Lord carried them (Deuteronomy 1:31). Neither their clothes nor their shoes wore out, nor did their feet swell (8:4; 29:5).

God also showed Himself as a Healer [Jehovah Rapha – Lord our Healer (Numbers 21:8)]. The children of Israel complained against Him because they were discouraged. Consequently, God sent fiery serpents which bit them. Many died. The people asked Moses to intercede on their behalf. God told Moses to make a fiery serpent of bronze and to set it on a pole. All who looked upon the serpent would not die, and so it was.

When the children of Israel needed assistance, God provided that also (El Hana-Eman – faithful God). Moses shared with God his feelings of inadequacy for the job assigned. God gave him Aaron as his assistant

(Exodus 4:14-16). During a battle with the Amalekites, when Moses would lift his hand, Israel would prevail and when he let down his hand, Amalek prevailed (17:11-12). Understandably, Moses' hand became tired, but Aaron and Hur sat him on a stone and each of them supported one of Moses' hands "until the going down of the sun." The assistance he needed was provided and the Amalekites were defeated. Jethro, Moses' father-in-law, saw that Moses and the people became weary due to long days of judging and waiting for judgments. He gave Moses counsel. Jethro told him to choose able men of integrity who feared God, to teach them the statutes, laws, behavior, and work they must do, and then to delegate some of the responsibilities to them (18:13-22). Moses learned that this was good counsel. Once again, assistance was given.

It was also in the wilderness that the Israelites learned to trust God for direction. Deuteronomy (8:15) informs us that it was God who led them "through the great and terrible wilderness." We are taught that He led them by a pillar of cloud during the day and a pillar of fire during the night (Exodus 13:21-22). He did not take either one from before the people.

In our wilderness sojourning, we can also learn things about God which we have not previously known. Sometimes it is just in this place that we learn He is all sufficient, that He has all the resources at His disposal and **will** provide what we need. There is nothing like being in a place of insufficient income, having little or no food, and having no foreseeable way of meeting those needs and then seeing God provide, many times through the most unexpected and unlikely ways. What a faith builder! However, if we had never been in that situation, we would not have been able to testify to the faithfulness of God and His all sufficiency. Or what is a greater faith builder in the healing power of God than to be sick, declared incurable by physicians, and through prayer be healed and then declared cured by the very doctors who pronounced you as practically dead! What can be more comforting than knowing you can ask God and He will lead you in the way you should go (Psalm 32:8; Isaiah 30:21)? Can there really be any doubt when you know that whatever assistance you require, God will put you in the path to receive it or provide someone to give the very help you need? Only when we are in places where an insufficiency exists and we have no means, but rather must totally depend on the Lord, can we learn Him in that manner. The wilderness is one of the most advantageous places to experience God in these ways.

There is a need for caution, however. Sometimes, help will come in the wilderness, but you must have discernment to determine from whence it came (Exodus 4:15-16). By whose authority does your help come? Does that which is supposed to be a help turn out to be a hindrance? Wilderness help must be rightly trained for wilderness conditions. When David was in a stronghold in the wilderness, on the run from Saul, he was joined by "mighty men of valor, men trained for battle, who could handle shield and spear, whose faces were like the faces of lions, and were as swift as gazelles on the mountain" (1st Chronicles 1:8). They progressively came to help David until they became "like the army of God" (vs. 22). They had what was needed and required for wilderness battle. The wilderness requires fighters who are able to stand the tests of time and hardship. They must be fighters who are not easily discouraged and ones who do not quickly become battle worn. They must also be fighters who are not thrown off by the conditions of the terrain. They must be intimate partners with God and warriors in prayer and the things of God. Even when David's own people came out to him, he did not just accept them without first questioning their motive (vs. 17). He said if they had come to help, he would unite with them, but if they had come to betray him, he asked that God's judgment be upon them. Many times in our wilderness frustration and desperation, we accept anybody or anything that comes along which even closely resembles help. Especially in this place we must seek God for direction. The betrayer of saints will send ones who will discourage you, try to sabotage the works of God, or who will put roadblocks on your path to deliverance. We can be assured, however, that if we sincerely, from our hearts seek God's counsel, He will preserve us from evil just as He did Nehemiah (6:11-13). He will send those who are able and will stand beside you to encourage you and help you get to the promised possession, the place God has for you.

IX.

Learning to Reverence God

The Lord told Moses He would come to him in a thick cloud and speak with him in a voice the people could hear also, in order to place belief in their heart forever (Exodus 19:10-15). He told him to bring them to the mountain to meet with Him. However, prior to the Israelites coming before the Lord, He instructed Moses to have them consecrate themselves. They could not come into His presence in their usual manner, but rather they had to prepare to meet the Lord.

Sam had not really lived his life for God. He had pretty much done as he pleased and only thought of God occasionally.

Then tragedy hit: there was a fire in his home, and it destroyed all he had. Having no one to turn to now and no resources of his own, Sam wanted to turn to God. But how could he possibly approach Him when he had treated Him so casually?

There is nothing like the wilderness to make us want to come near to God. The felt desperation of that desolate place calls forth and incites within us a great need to "see Him," to experience Him in an unusual way. The children of Israel had seen the works of God and knew Him by the move of His hand, but now they needed and were going to witness and learn Him in another way. The wilderness can create within us an urgency to realize Him in a way which exceeds the ordinary. Many times, because of the intensity, the heat of this passion to "know" Him, we forget Who God is, His nature. We forget that He is holy and must be revered, and that if we are to approach Him, it must be in an esteemed way. God must be approached with a mind toward His holiness and complete sovereignty. We have to be prepared for that encounter. Just as the Israelites could not come to Him in a disrespectful, unholy way, neither are we to come in that manner. They had to be consecrated (Exodus 19:10); that is they had to be set apart from the ordinary and dedicated to the extraordinary, and so must we. Their clothes had to be cleaned just as Sam will have to become clean through acceptance of the atoning work of Christ and repentance from his old ways. He will need to become a new creation. For a season, the Israelites had to abstain from fleshly pleasure and satisfaction so that they might concentrate on meeting the Lord (vs. 15). They would later learn that holiness requires a life of sacrifices. Sam will also have to relinquish non-ordained, sinful, flesh satisfying behavior, and he too must learn that his life will have to become one of being led by the Spirit of God.

Approaching God without reverence is a serious offense. When He presented Himself on top of the mountain, the Israelites were afraid (Exodus 20:20), but Moses told them that He had come so "that His fear might be upon you, so that you may not sin." We are instructed by the word of God that "the fear of the Lord is the beginning of knowledge" (Proverbs 1:7). When Korah, Dathan, and Abiram rebelled against Moses and Aaron, God's spokesmen, the Lord did a "new thing" and opened the mouth of the earth which swallowed them with their households (Numbers 16:1-32). The things of God are to be respected. When one rebels against that which God has established, the rebelling person is revolting against God Himself (1st Samuel 8:4-

8) and is consequently inviting the results of that action into his/her life. The children of Israel were cautioned to remember how they had provoked the wrath of God in the wilderness, and that He was angry enough to destroy them as well as Aaron, but Moses interceded on their behalf (Deuteronomy 9:7-8, 14, 25-29) and their lives were spared. Even the New Testament warns that if a saint continues in behavior that brings dishonor to the name of Christ, that saint may not be allowed to live (1st Corinthians 5:1-5).

Why is it mandatory and what does it mean to reverence God? Reverence is given to Him because He is reverent; that is, He is sacred and holy. To reverence God means to come to Him as One whose character is such. It means to show respect for and submission to Him. Most assuredly, it implies a humbling of self before the One Who made the heavens and the earth and everything in them, and Who reigns and rules over all that exists.

Once we have prepared our hearts to reverentially meet the Lord, we have placed ourselves in a position to be instructed by Him. He is more than willing to teach us; actually, He delights in it. He has a planned purpose for each of our lives and He has promised that He will instruct us in the way we should go (Psalm 2:8). If we have rightly prepared ourselves to meet Him, we will be in a humbled frame of mind, a posture that enables us to receive what God requires, to receive teaching from Him. It was in the wilderness that Moses first received his mandate from God, his assignment (Exodus 3-4). Throughout the wilderness journey, God continued to direct him. Once God directs, we are held accountable for obedience. Psalm 95 reminds us that we must not rebel against God as the Israelites did in the wilderness.

They rebelled to the extent that He swore His wrath upon them and they were not allowed to enter His rest (vs. 7-11). Rather we are to realize that obedience is better than sacrifice (1st Samuel 15:22). He has said He will not withhold any good thing from us if we walk uprightly before Him (Psalm 84:11), which means if we walk obediently.

When we have a heartfelt desire to please God, we are concerned about knowing exactly what He wants and requires of us. Because we love Him and, therefore, reverence Him, we **want** to obey His commands. One might ask, "How can I know if I'm doing what He wants?" God is a perfect Father. What parent would deny his/her child the knowledge needed to obey if that parent knew the child sincerely wanted to be obedient? If we, being human and of a sinful nature would so instruct our children, how much more will our heavenly

Father, Who is perfect, instruct those who genuinely desire to heed His voice? No, He will not leave us on our own to figure it out; He will guide us with His eye (Psalm 32:8). We have the wonderful privilege of prayer, and we have the Spirit of God living within us. He is there to lead and guide us. As we pray, He will repeat to us only that which He has heard from the Father (John 16:13-14). Consequently, we can and will have an inner assurance that we have heard the will of God. When He gave Moses His assignment concerning the building of the "Tent of Meeting," Moses was left without a doubt as to what God desired. He was specific and detailed in His instructions, showing Moses exactly how all was to be done (Exodus 25:9). To assure that things would be accomplished in the way He wanted, God filled certain men with His Spirit, "in wisdom, in understanding, in knowledge, and in all manner of workmanship" to build and design all that was instructed (Exodus 31:1-11). When we earnestly seek the will of God, He will make it plain to us because He is a rewarder of those who diligently seek Him (Hebrews 11:6). We can learn to submit to His will, to reverence Him.

X.

Learning to Overcome Enemies

Pharaoh had shown himself to be an enemy of the children of Israel. After years of forced labor by his hands, he had been compelled, by the demonstrations of the Lord, to grant them their freedom. Nevertheless, in spite of all he had seen, Pharaoh's heart was hardened and he pursued them into the wilderness (Exodus 14:3-13). Upon realizing his pursuit, the children of Israel cried out because they were afraid; the sea was in front of them and Pharaoh was pressing hard behind them. They didn't know what to do. Moses told them to stand still and witness what the Lord would accomplish. He assured them that their enemies, the Egyptians, would be destroyed and they would be seen "again no more forever" (vs. 13).

Sariah was constantly getting into arguments with her husband. She hated those times, but no matter how much she resolved that she would not argue, her words just seemed to have a mind of their own. They were spoken before she would even realize what was taking place. Part of the problem was she could not stand being treated this way, and her husband always seemed to behave in a manner which provoked Sariah to respond as she did. Her friends agreed that she had a right to be offended.

Conditions that exist in the wilderness increase the possibilities for overcoming enemies, those things that hinder us and serve as obstacles in our walk with God. When we are alone, hungry, frustrated, perplexed, or bewildered, our true nature will oftentimes come forth. It is in this place that we see of what we are truly made. We discover those things which are plaguing our conduct. For example, we are quite often willing to serve when we are feeling happy, all is going well and there is no pressure on our time. But at the end of a day which has been filled with challenges, unexpected interruptions, and constant demands, are we still willing to keep our neighbor's child overnight because the parents have told us they **desperately** need a "time out"? Will we take the time to listen to that person who needs to talk about troubles s/he is having? These are tests that let us know what is really inside of us, what the true enemies to our servanthood are.

Sometimes we will keep our commitment and perform our acts of service, but tarnish our witness and forfeit our joy by complaining. This was frequently the response of the children of Israel; when trouble or discomfort arose, they grumbled and complained. The wilderness, because it is a seat of despair, tends to create within us a desire to tell others our troubles and grievances because we want to get their sympathy and we want them to affirm our position, just as Sariah had obviously done by sharing her circumstances with her friends. We want to be validated in our "rightness" and feelings of being "put upon." Through grumbling and complaining, we seek to confirm our right to feel as we do, and thereby we show that we have not developed a servant's heart. The <u>enemy of **offense**</u> surfaces.

There is also another adversary that may show itself in the wilderness. Frequently it is hidden, but generally lies at the heart of the more obvious foes, that is the <u>enemy of **pride**</u>. Pride always centers on self, either in the form of actions or words that cause us to feel devalued, or in the form of actions or words that cause us to feel esteemed. Whatever the case, the result is a focus on "me." Pride brings with it feelings of being "put down", depression, bitterness, rebellion, anger and high-mindedness, and it is often easily offended: because I have this high opinion of myself [thinking more highly of myself than I ought (Romans 12:3)], I can quickly feel I have been belittled. I then become depressed and bitter toward the one who I think has caused me to feel this way. The more I think of what has been done, I become angrier and, consequently, I retaliate against the one who has committed the offense.

Built into these attitudes are selfish thoughts such as "**I** deserve better than this," "**I** have a right to not be treated this way," or "How could she/he treat **me** like this?" Plainly, at the core of these ruminations is a focus on "I" or "me."

Perhaps not as clear as the above, but having just as strong an influence are ideas about the positive thoughts, feelings, or behavior we believe people will have toward us because of some perceived good deed we have done, something we have accomplished, or because of the accomplishment of someone close to us. These too are prideful. (If we would see them as they are, as blessings from God and as the result of His love and grace, feelings of thankfulness would ensue and praise and honor would be given to Him. All credit would be attributed to Him.)

Because we are in a vulnerable position in the wilderness, it is fertile ground for thoughts and feelings of pride to come forth, sometimes in less than obvious ways. Think for a moment of how the shame we may associate with our situation frequently causes us to want to hide our true state. This feeling usually results from pride due to the value we have placed on and projected about ourselves. Our perceived self is at risk of being diminished. For example, when you're in the wilderness of destitution, will you accept that much needed help when it's available or offered? An even greater test for pride might be to ask for help when needed. Or, when there is an invitation to receive prayer for those who are in the wilderness of falleness, will you go to the altar? This too is a litmus test for pride.

All these feelings begin with and take root in what we tell ourselves about the things which happen in our lives. When we attribute or in some way connect esteemed events to our abilities or characteristics, pride is the result.

Also during challenging times in the wilderness, we may be faced with another <u>enemy: the sin of **second thoughts**</u>. This occurs when we look back and wish to return to those days when we remember things as being better. Especially during trying times, we may vacillate between trusting and doubt, belief and unbelief, joy and sorrow, peace and anxiety. It is at these forks in the road that we are confronted with our tendency to retreat to the past, to the "comfort zone." When the children of Israel were faced with the danger of Pharaoh's pursuit, they first cried out to the Lord, but shortly after, they complained against Moses, telling him it would have been better for them to have served the Egyptians than to die in the wilderness (Exodus 14:10-12). They looked back. But after they had crossed the Red Sea, they sang songs of praises to God (15:1-2). When things are going well, we tend to be hopeful, expectant, and optimistic. But it is when the course of travel goes in an unwanted direction that our real or hidden nature is brought to light. There is a song which lyrics read, "Where He leads I will follow. I will go with Him all the way." Eagerly, we grasp these words and assume that we are singing and meaning them from our hearts. However, when we hit that rut in the road of His leading, or upon following Him we happen upon terrain which appears to be untravelable at most and treacherous at the least, we begin to contemplate that "home place" or the place from which we departed: "At least that was better than having a terrible accident and perhaps killing myself." How quickly we forget why we initially left that place, that it was situated in a low area and was susceptible to flooding. How quickly we forget the constant fear we had there and the real danger of perishing, or at the least losing all we had, that existed in that place. Just like the children of Israel, we soon forget that in Egypt we were enslaved. Memories are always more favorable than the reality when it was actually experienced. The pleasant memories surface readily, but we have to remind ourselves of the things which consistently caused us to want to leave. But just as Moses told the Israelites, if you will not be afraid, remain for now in this place by realizing and coming to terms with the things facing you, and allow the Lord to show you yourself, you will see the salvation of the Lord, and He can accomplish it so that you will never see your "enemies" again. This is one of the reasons you are here. You cannot afford for your enemies to remain intact. As long as they are in your life, they will pose as major obstacles on your journey. Psalm 23 reminds us that there is a table prepared before you in the presence of these enemies. Realize it is there and partake of its holdings. The One Who has prepared it is there to show that through Him you can overcome.

XI.

Learning the Consequences of Unrepentant Sin

Moses sent twelve men to spy out the land of Canaan, the Israelites' Promised Land (Numbers 13). The spies confirmed what the Lord had said about the land, but they also put fear into the hearts of the people by describing the inhabitants as strong and like giants. As a result the people refused to enter Canaan; they doubted God would do what He said. Because of their doubts and complaints against Him, God assigned the Israelites to wander in the wilderness for forty years.

Paul's wife had been unfaithful to him and he had consequently separated from her. Although she had hurt him deeply, he had hopes that the marriage could be reconciled. During the interim, he found himself lonely and felt that since his wife had already broken the marriage vows, he was free to pursue a relationship himself, and so he did. He did not perceive this to be wrong, therefore, when they would reunite, surely his wife would understand.

Sometimes, we find ourselves in the wilderness because of planned and unrepentant sin. More times than not, it is due to giving in to our carnal desires. Just like Paul, we may have been hurt deeply, and in our pain we try to justify a wrongful action that we think will make us feel better. Ultimately, we will not feel better because sin eventually steals our joy, kills our spirits, and destroys our testimony and the fruitfulness of our lives. Consistent sin only multiplies itself; satisfying the body makes it want more of the same.

Like the children of Israel, we may be in the wilderness because we have complained against God and doubted Him, and because of that doubt, rebelled against stepping into our promised possession when He has directed us to do so. All of us, at some point in our lives, have doubted. Although doubting is a human commonality, we are not to surrender to it. God has shown us that we can bring everything to Him, even our doubts (Mark 9:23-24). He is willing to reward the smallest particle of faith (Matthew 17:20).

Usually doubting and its companion, complaining against God, come when we are trusting in ourselves and not in His power. Sin is then birthed. Because of unbelief, we do not do what God has instructed us and therefore, we sin because to disobey God is sin.

The wilderness affords us the brokenness that is needed to confront our sin, confess it before the Lord, and let His forgiveness allow us to forgive ourselves. However, it is not enough just to confess the sin without repenting. To repent means to "change one's mind or purpose, always in the N.T., involving a change for the better . . . ." (*Vine's Expository Dictionary*, 1997). Therefore, confession must be accompanied by heartfelt desire and determination to turn away from the sin and by kneeling before God with a remorse spirit and belief in His Spirit to enable us to live a life of holiness. We are assured that "if we confess our sins, He is faithful and just to forgive us our sins and to cleanse us from all unrighteousness" (1 John 1:9). To continue in sin brings sure spiritual death, but repenting of it can make "roads in the wilderness and rivers in the desert" (Isaiah 43: 19).

    Do not allow the enemy to convince you that what you have done is so terrible God could never forgive and accept you into His family. The reality is that before you were even born, He knew everything there ever would be to know about you. The things you have done are no surprise to Him, and they were already taken into account when He set His love on you, when He chose and established you as His own. You are now free to confess everything before the One Who knows all things. He is more than willing to forgive a repentant heart. As a matter of fact, He has been waiting for you to get here. What could be better than coming forth from this place of desolation as a "new you," having been cleansed from the old. Repentance allows us to begin again. It brings refreshing and newness. These conditions are perfect for making "new wine" and "new wineskins."

XII.

Learning to Die

After the children of Israel refused to enter the Promised Land, the "carcasses" of those twenty years of age and older, those who had complained against the Lord in unbelief, fell in the wilderness; that is, they died there (Numbers 13:29). Those with the old habits were not allowed to enter into the new land.

John and Martha's marriage had been rocky for a long time. There were frequent arguments and consistent tension between them. Each thought of his/her needs more than the other's and neither felt his/her needs were being met. Both had been members of a Bible teaching church since their adolescent years; therefore, they knew the difference between right and wrong. However, each believed him/herself to be right. Neither John nor Martha would readily concede to being in error. Pride and self-centeredness were at the heart of much of their troubles. Very rarely did either think of being a blessing or of reflecting Christ to the other.

The children of Israel had barely left Egypt before they began to develop a habit of rebelling against God. Their journey in the wilderness vacillated between praise and obedience and complaining, bitterness, and rebellion. When things were going the way they wanted, or when God answered their request in the way they desired, their response would be praise, worship, and commitment to Him. However, as soon as conditions became adverse, or when they found themselves in a challenging situation, they returned to complaining against Him, to bitterness toward their leaders, and to rebelling against the ways of God. These reactions showed that in spite of all they had seen, the Israelites did not fully believe God; they did not have a sustaining faith, the kind of faith that would keep them in spite of the circumstances they faced. It also illustrated that they held their lives, wants, comfort, and expectations in higher regard than they held God, and He would not have an unbelieving, "stiff-necked" (Exodus 33:5), self-centered generation going into the new land. Things that contaminated the purifying product had to be cast out during the refining process; they must be destroyed.

All the synoptic gospels record Jesus as saying that to follow Him requires denying **self** and losing **one's life** (Matthew 16:24-25; Mark:34-35; Luke:23-24). He declared that we can not become bondservants (under subjection) for Him until we have put to death our self-centered interests and concerns. Only then can we sincerely begin to live our lives for Him. Paul writes that when we committed our lives to Christ, our old lifestyles, our "flesh with its passion and desires," were crucified with Him (Romans 6:6; Galatians 5:24); they died with Him. That is why Paul could proclaim he had been crucified with Christ to the extent that he no longer lived, but rather Christ lived in him (Galatians 2:20). He had "died" to his old ways and had forsaken living his life for himself. Being totally committed to another requires this sacrifice.

How can self be denied and life be lost except through dying to both? To die means the object passes "out of existence" and the person becomes "indifferent" to the dead thing (*Webster's Collegiate Dictionary*, 1983). Therefore, when we have died to something, the matter no longer exists for us; consequently, we have become detached from it and it ceases to be the object of our focus or care. However, the "death" does not occur in one moment of transformation. As we enjoin ourselves to Christ's service, the dying process begins. Our focus begins to shift away from us and toward serving Him. There is a change in our passions. Our primary concerns become whether or not we are pleasing Him by doing His will, whether or not we are fulfilling His purpose for our lives, and whether or not we are contributing to the Kingdom of Heaven. The goals of the Kingdom become our goals and the driving motivation of our lives. His desires are our desires. We awake each morning with the attitude of a soldier reporting for duty: "What are my orders for today?" We begin to have tunnel vision, vision which looks only and continuously to Him for direction. Our selves and our lives are being mortified.

The terrain of the wilderness is very helpful in achieving this "death" of self and hence loss of life; that is, it helps us to become indifferent to the self-centered and self-seeking life. Because the region includes steep places, to climb them will force us to throw off weights which are devoid of value and are compromising our energy. In this position, the things which are the most important become clearer. We learn that the things on which we have placed so much earthly significance have little, if any, eternal worth, and therefore can be discarded. We understand the only possessions which will stand the tests of time are those we have committed to Christ's service for His purposes and those used in His name. Pleasing ourselves and our self satisfaction usually do not fall into these categories, and therefore, become of little, if any, consideration to us; they begin to die.

The wilderness also facilitates the dying process through its bareness. Because of its sparseness, we learn to distinguish between those things which can be done without and the ones which are absolutely necessary for survival. We learn many of the things we previously believed to be a necessity for our existence are not essential at all, but we come to know it is impossible to live without God, we cannot flourish without Him. This newly found truth makes it easier to discard the weights which are unnecessary. Through the direness of these circumstances, we learn all that is truly required is the Lord Himself. In this place where "water" (the Spirit) may **appear** to be scarce and "food" (the presence of our Lord) may be **perceived** as limited, we learn these are indeed the most critical elements for our daily living. All else fades as we face the reality that our survival **really** depends on Him, as we compare all other desires to our need for Him. This realization can cause us to lovingly submit and therein become less and less important to ourselves. We become more willing to give up all things to follow Christ, and then we die daily (1st Corinthians 15:31). During this process we become true followers of Christ.

To be a true follower requires one to submit to a leader. Therefore, if we are to follow Christ with our entire heart, it will require relinquishing our desires to go in a specific direction. It will require the surrender of our plans, hopes, and dreams and instead submit to the will of God for our lives. Sometimes your desires will coincide with God's, but even when they do not, He has a way of increasing your appetite for that which He is calling you to do. You may in the beginning feel less than eager about His plans, but after a period of time, you will find yourself wanting, excited about and gladly looking forward to that very thing. The dying process continues.

As we truly die to ourselves, our focus is no longer on the "mys" of our existence: my rights, my possessions, my happiness, my pleasure, etc. Feelings take a back seat and are made to line up with the will of God. Pleasing Him becomes the central focus and joy of life, and following Him becomes our pleasure. Again, this growth does not occur at once, but rather increases as we obey God. The joy of obeying Him becomes addictive, and the more of Him we experience, the more of Him we want to experience. Obedience becomes our pattern. When we have arrived at this point, we can truly proclaim as Paul: "I have been crucified with Christ; it is no longer I who live, but Christ lives in me; and the life which I now live in the flesh I live by faith in the Son of God, who loved me and gave Himself for me" (Galatians 2:20). You will come to realize the truth of the scripture which informs, "In Him we live and move and have our being . . ." (Acts 17:28).

XIII.

Learning to Listen

Moses, as well as the children of Israel, had learned that God would speak to them. He had spoken to Moses on numerous occasions (Numbers 1:1; 9:1, for examples) and He had also spoken within the hearing of the Israelites (Exodus 19:19; 20:22). In the process of hearing His voice, they were learning to obey God (Numbers 9:23). They were also learning that not doing what He commanded reaped serious consequences (Deuteronomy 9).

Jonathan felt as if he was just spinning his wheels. Everything in his life seemed to be going wrong. His marriage was not what he had dreamed and fantasized it would be. His children seemed to be going in a direction opposite of the one he had hoped for their lives. His job no longer brought him any satisfaction. There was no real joy in his life except his relationship with the Lord, but even there, he felt confused. He didn't know what to do with his life. He loved God and wanted to be doing work in the Kingdom, but didn't know what. How could he find out? How could he know why he was put on this earth, what he was put here to do? Shouldn't he be doing **something?** *Shouldn't he be initiating something? How could he arrive at a place where his life would have some meaning?*

It is a fact that God speaks to His people. He has been doing so since there have been a people to whom He wanted to speak, and He will continue to speak throughout eternity. God is our Father, and if we have earthly fathers who must speak to their children, desire to do so, and delight in speaking to them, why would our heavenly Father Who is perfect not also view it as a necessity to speak to His children, wish to do so, and take pleasure in talking with us? The fact that He left a written word makes the case for the importance of Him communicating with us.

It is not God's will for us not to know His words or to be confused about them. His sheep hear His voice (John 10:27) and He is not the author of confusion (1st Corinthians 14:33). He would not have us to be unsure about His directions and paths for our lives because it is written He "will instruct you and teach you in the way you should go; I will guide you with My eye" (Psalm 32:8). The wilderness, however, can be a confusing place because during this time, we often feel we're on a journey which must be traveled alone. There is no one to tell us where we are going, and the paths and the highways leading to our destination are hidden from view by the trees or desert sands. Additionally, the territory can be filled with unknown dangers, and terror can fill our hearts. The darkness of the nights brings added fear to our already present confusion. But here, in this place of aloneness, the conditions are prime for realizing the presence of God. It is here we can turn to Him; there is no one else and He is always present. We can learn to talk with Him, learn to listen to Him, and by listening, learn to recognize His voice.

Because the Spirit of the Lord is always with us, He is always ready to listen when we cry out to Him, but within the wilderness, His attentiveness is nothing short of astounding. Psalm 34:18 explains He "is near to those who have a broken heart, and saves such as have a contrite spirit." Our Father is full of compassion for us. He understands every one of our feelings, and His desire is to help. If you allow Him, He will walk you through this time. Listen for Him. "The Lord will hear when I call to Him" (Psalm 4:3). "He will be very gracious to you at the sound of your cry; when he hears it, He will answer you" (Isaiah 30:19b). He is only a thought away, and when we turn our mind to Him, we will find Him in the place where He always is: wherever we are, and ready to speak to us. We are never alone. Because He is with us, no matter what the situation or circumstance, God knows all about it and it is under His sovereign control. Nothing can happen to us unless it passes by Him first; only then is it allowed to come to us. Job's narrative account enlightens us to that fact (Job 1:10-12; 2:4-6).

    Sometimes the wilderness is so overwhelming we lose sight of the reality of God being in control of our life events. Because we view things as being out of control, we assume that they must be with God also. But He has **promised** He will make **all** things work for our good (Romans 8:28), no matter how unpleasant or how disappointing they may appear to us. During this time of darkness and confusion, He will reward you if you seek Him diligently (Hebrews 11:6). Moses learned this during the wilderness wanderings (Deuteronomy 9:20, 25). Time and time again, he sought the Lord regarding things for which he needed direction or intervention. God always answered him, and He will answer us also.

In this domain of stillness and quietness, the ultimate position for hearing God, we can be given our assignments, made aware of our purpose. Each of us has a sacred calling and a purpose for our lives. Since eternity God has had individual assignments with each one of us in mind (Jeremiah 29:11). Before we were ever formed in the womb, He knew us (Jeremiah 1:5).

We may discover that purpose in the wilderness. It was in the wilderness that Aaron learned he was to be Moses' assistant (Exodus 4:27). That was the beginning of his life in service to God. How little did he know he would become a priest to the Israelites. Furthermore, his sons received their assignments in the wilderness and became priests to the people. Bezalel and Aholiab were commissioned in the wilderness as well (Exodus 31:2-11). They had the divine assignment to build the first temple, the Tabernacle of Meeting, and all its furnishings. It would be the place where God would reside with his people. This Tabernacle would also be the framework for all Jewish temples to come. These assignments, in combination, set the perimeters for worshipping God and how we are to approach Him. What commissions! Yours too may await you, but you must be listening.

The best way to know with certainty your purpose and God's plan for you is to ask Him to reveal it. What better place to seek His answer than in this place of quiet repose, the place where you are more likely to be attentive to His voice. Concerning this matter, it is a must that you hear **from God**. It is quite common for others to share their perception of our gifts, and we are oftentimes eager to hear it. But while their perceptions may be accurate, only God can definitely inform and determine what He has placed within you. When He has confirmed it, there will be no error. God will bless what **He** has purposed. Therefore, it is crucial that you do not move ahead or outside of Him. Listen for His directions. Moses learned that lesson in the wilderness, and this knowledge caused Him to pen: "If Your Presence does not go with us, do not bring us up from here" (Exodus 33:15). None of us wants to find ourselves in a place where God has not ordained or commissioned us to be, a place where He will take a non-interference stance. When He has sanctioned something, it is bound to prosper, but when we proceed on our own, failure is a real probability. So it behooves us to consult Him, then wait and listen for His answer and instructions. The children of Israel were led by a pillar of cloud by day and one of fire by night, which were the leadings of the Spirit of God. They did not move unless the pillars moved. They were completely dependent on the leading of God. And we must be also. He will speak. Incline your ear to hear.

XIV.

Learning to Love

After God gave Moses the Ten Commandments, the children of Israel were told they must observe all God had commanded them to do (Deuteronomy 8:1-2). They were told the Lord had led them in the wilderness those forty years "to humble you and test you, to know what was in your heart, whether you would keep His commandments or not" (vs. 2). His clear directive was: "Therefore you shall love the Lord your God, and keep His charge, His statutes, His judgments, and His commandments always" (Deuteronomy 11:1). He explained that He expected love from them because He was not speaking to ones who did not know or had not seen His works, but rather to those who had witnessed the mighty Hand of God through His many acts (vs. 2-7). In the wilderness, the Israelites began to realize their love would be shown by keeping the commandments, and that this love would intensify as they continually experienced God and obeyed Him.

Mason and Carissa had only been married two months. Already they both were questioning if this marriage was going to work. Arguments seemed to be more frequent than they had imagined or thought should be taking place between two people who love each other. What had happened to the fervent love they both felt only months ago? Carissa remembered the wedding vows: he had promised to take care of her, to cherish and honor her, and to respect her above all others. In return, she had vowed to honor, respect, trust and cherish him above anyone else. Mason was also thinking about Carissa. He held memories of her as being peaceable, and as consistently showing acts of love and kindness toward him. Both wondered what had happened. Why were there so many problems now? Did they truly know what love really involves? As they both pondered the situation, they were drawn to recall what had initially attracted them to each other. This "soul searching" made them realize that those same qualities were still there, but they were simply failing to see them. Each then became willing and determined to show the other love by focusing on her/his endearing qualities and on how each could please the other and meet the other's needs. Both determined to be a blessing in the life of the other; they would learn how to truly love.

When we are in the wilderness, we can be very vulnerable. Our emotions are not reliable indicators of true reality. Most often things appear to be worse than they actually are or they appear to be irresolvable, to have no possible, favorable end. Fear of what will happen grips us. Many times we are so oppressed by our circumstances that our perceptions are lost on everything except the despair we now feel. We have difficulty thinking beyond the moment. However, if we involve ourselves in a reexamination, we find prior to the crisis, it has been relatively easy to love God, but the fire of the trial is testing our real love. It is revealing what is in our heart, the purposes for which we serve Him, and whether our commitment is genuine and long term. There is no denying that it is easier to feel and show love when things are prospering and going well, but now that trouble is at our door, where do we stand?

The wilderness was the test for the Israelites. Time and time again they showed what was at their central core. Their pattern was to rejoice and praise when things were going well, and to turn their hearts away from God when things became challenging. Their love was conditional and unstable; it depended on their pleasure or displeasure with His actions and on their circumstances. They quickly forgot the acts of love God had shown toward them. Easily their minds returned to the days they perceived as being good (Numbers 11:5), the days before they had experienced the goodness of God, true goodness. How quickly they forgot they had been slaves in Egypt and that they had cried out to the Lord because of their oppression (Exodus 2:7). They had forgotten the extent to which He had gone to bring about their deliverance, how His grace, mercy, and compassion had now caused them to be free. Their heart was being revealed.

We sometimes marvel at the children of Israel. We are amazed that God could have done so much, yet they could so quickly forget. We are astonished at their continuing fears and doubts. We are perplexed by their grumbling and complaining. But we are not so different. We readily share our testimonies about the goodness of God when He has healed us or a loved one. We cannot wait to share the good news of how he enabled us to get the car we needed or the house we wanted. We spread the word about receiving that job or job promotion immediately. But when we are in the pit of our despair, can we just as readily share the goodness of God? Can we talk about His kindness, mercy, and compassion? Will we take a bold and confident stand on our trust in Him knowing that nothing can happen to us that He has not allowed? Do we eagerly anticipate the good that He has promised will come out of this? Are we willing to and can we truthfully declare like Job that though He slays us, we will continue to trust in Him (Job 13:15)? Can we boldly proclaim as the Hebrew boys did that we know our God is able to deliver us from the trial, but even if He does not we will serve no other god (Daniel 3:17)? Do our hearts assure us that we truly love Him?

The wildernesses of life test true love. *Vine's Expository Dictionary* (1997) informs that love can **only** be known by the actions it brings forth. Therefore, there is no love if it is not accompanied by actions. True love is shown to be lacking when you declare your love for Someone (God), but when difficulty arises, you look back toward your former loves (old life), or you turn forward toward a new love (new carnal desires) and then distance yourself from your present love (God). Perhaps it was only infatuation from the beginning. To be sure, there are times in relationships when feelings of distance are experienced. But, when the love is true, you know deep inside that your love for the person remains, and after a short period, those negative feelings do disappear and you are once again revived by that love.

The wilderness which is consumed by overgrown foliage (confusion), giant trees which are preventing you from seeing your way (problems), limited sources of refreshing water (comfort and relief), wild animals that threaten your very life (actual conditions), and terrors that keep you in constant fear (feelings) can and will test what is in your heart. However, once you come to the realization that you have not been overtaken by any of these obstacles, but rather have overcome all the hurdles placed before you, and when you realize that God has been with you every step of the way, that it was Him and Him alone Who brought you through, you will discover love for Him. You find you love Him because He has loved you in spite of yourself. His love has not been based on your actions and behavior; it has not been conditional. He loves you because He is and you are. You love Him because He loved you before you could ever love Him. He loved you before you were born. You will also discover a desire to please Him, which entails obeying Him and loving those whom He loves. You will find yourself learning to love what He loves and hate those things which are offensive to Him. You will find yourself wanting to demonstrate your love. You will have come to know you have life because He lives. Your love is now real.

XV.

Learning to Build (The Temple)

After God had given Moses His judgments and instructions concerning the way of life the Israelites were to follow, He told Moses to come to Him on the mountain, whereon He gave him the instructions for building a tabernacle in the wilderness (Exodus 20-30). It would be the place where the Lord would dwell with them (Exodus 25:8) and consequently it would be their central place of worship. The tabernacle would also be a place whereupon they could look and remember the Lord their God and His instructions to them. It was to assume even more significance for them because the

Israelites were to have a personal investment in its construction: all who were willing in their hearts were to bring offerings which would be used as building materials. Therefore, each would have something invested in the place where the Lord resided; each would have contributed to the place where He would be worshipped.

Alvin has had a pretty good life. He has always had a good job, allowing him to get the things he needed and many of the things he wanted. His walk with the Lord had been pretty smooth also; nothing catastrophic or traumatic had challenged or posed as obstacles on his road toward heaven. But one day he received the news that his company was closing and he found himself without a job. How would he pay his bills? How would he provide for his family? As the weeks passed and the end of his unemployment was in view, Alvin was confronted with what to do about his financial commitments to the Lord. Could he possibly continue to tithe and give offerings? Could he and would he really trust God? Could he part with that which was now so valued and needed?

The word "tabernacle" is defined as a dwelling (*Vine's Expository Dictionary*, 1997). As explained above, the tabernacle in the wilderness was to be the place where God would dwell with his people, Israel. The children of Israel could look toward the tabernacle and remember their God. They could look toward it and recall what He had done for them, how He had so mightily delivered them out of Egypt, how He had provided for them during their wilderness wanderings, His provisions of the manna from heaven, and how neither their clothes nor their shoes had worn out (Deuteronomy 29:5). Moses and the priests placed their concerns before God in the tabernacle. Their answers and comfort came from His dwelling place. Residing with them in the wilderness would help the children of Israel learn He could be trusted; they could depend on Him. They could know Him to be reliable based on their past experiences with God. When the Israelites looked there and really considered their history, they could realize He had never failed them. The greatness of their God would help them understand they had been honored by being asked and had been blessed to be able to contribute to the place of His dwelling. A God so great surely did not need or have to have what they had to offer to build His dwelling place, but He had allowed it so the contents of their hearts might be revealed.

The tabernacle remained with the Israelites throughout their wilderness sojourn. It was a constant reminder of God and His presence. The greatness of the structure represented the fact that He was larger than their lives. Its central location would remind them that He was in the middle of their lives, their situations and their circumstances. He was neither to be forgotten nor be ignored. No matter what came upon them, He was greater than any situation they would face. They were to remember that it was He who went before them by day and night, and when necessary, He was the shield of protection that separated them from their enemies (Exodus 14:19-20).

During the times of our wilderness sojourning, we must also build a symbolic tabernacle which will serve the same purposes for us as it did for the children of Israel. Board by board (Bible chapter by Bible chapter) and animal skin by animal skin (verse by verse) we must construct our "tabernacle" as a place of refuge, strength, remembrance, promise, faith and encouragement. The sparseness and lean times of the wilderness pose a real challenge to remembering the goodness and workings of God. We are hard pressed to recall His provisions of the past, His continual presence, faithfulness, and His trustworthiness. We also will have to bring our "freewill offerings," the situations from which we have been delivered, His provisions during our times of need, His presence during intense times of loneliness and despair, and His peace during turbulent times (in other words, our testimonies), and we will construct a special and definite place where we can realize God's constant presence. It will serve as that place toward which we look during times when we are confronted by the dangers of the wilderness, when we are faced with doubt, discouragement, fear, anxiety, loneliness, despair, and insecurity. We can run into that place when we feel afraid, threatened, weak, alone, and without hope. It is there wherein we can be renewed and provided with what we need to continue the journey. God is faithful. He never leaves or forsakes us. In the midst of our calamities, there we will find Him. We must remember that nothing can happen to us that He has not allowed, and He has promised to make it work for our good. Because we trust in Him, He will keep us in perfect peace if our minds stay on Him (Isaiah 26:3). The challenge is to keep our minds on Him. This "tabernacle" can help us keep our focus. His word, our relationship with Him, and our communication with Him will provide the assurance of safety, the realization of protection and provision, and the comfort of direction and guidance. "Yea though I walk through the valley of the shadow of death, I will fear no evil for you are with me" (Psalm 23:4). Your "tabernacle" can be a constant reminder of this truth.

XVI.

Learning to Possess the Land

The children of Israel were told if they would keep all the commandments of the Lord, He would give them the Promised Land by driving out all the nations before them, nations greater and mightier than they (Deuteronomy 11:22). He said He would put dread and fear of them upon all the land wherein they walked (vs. 24), and no one would be able to stand against them because the Lord their God would go before them. They would conquer all that would hinder them from taking possession of the land. The only requirement for the

Israelites was to believe God and to take control of that which had been given.

Allison loved the Lord with all her heart. There was a place in Him where she wanted to be. She had read Habakkuk 3:19: "The Lord God is my strength; He will make my feet like deer's feet, and He will make me walk on my high hills," and she was claiming it as her own. How could she get to this place? What did she need to do?

God promised Abraham his descendents would be given land "from the river of Egypt to the great Euphrates…" (Genesis 15:18). He also said, however, that before they would acquire the inheritance, these descendents would be afflicted and would be servants in a strange land for four hundred years (vs. 13). But He said He would judge that nation, and the descendents would come out with great possessions (vs. 14). The children of Israel were the recipients of the foretold affliction and servitude, but additionally they were heirs to the promise. Now four hundred and forty years later, they were on the verge of receiving the promise, the Promised Land.

Allison also had a promise: "Now this is the confidence that we have in Him, that if we ask anything according to His will, He hears us. And if we know that He hears us, whatever we ask, we know that we have the petitions that we have asked of Him" (1 John 5:14-15). God's word is His will. All Allison has to do is believe His word and allow it to begin to activate the faith to believe she will have what she desires. She can be confident because what she is seeking pleases God and is His will.

Allison and the Israelites have something in common: both must take possession of the promise in order to make it their own. But to assume ownership requires obedience:

> Now it shall come to pass, if you diligently obey the voice of the Lord your God, to observe carefully all His commandments which I command you today, that the Lord your God will set you high above all the nations of the earth. And all these blessings shall come upon you and overtake you, because you obey the voice of the Lord your God… (Deuteronomy 28:1-2).

"If anyone loves Me, he will keep My word; and My Father will love him, and We will come to him and make our home with him" (John 14:23).

"If you abide in Me and My words abide in you, you will ask what you desire, and it shall be done for you" (John 15:7).

Many people want the promises of God, but do not want a relationship with Him. They are not willing to pray, do not read His word, or follow His commands. Others want the prize, but they are not willing to go the distance the race requires. As long as the road in the wilderness is easy or does not pose too many challenges or hardships, they continue, but as soon as the way becomes difficult, they turn back, thinking the cost to be too great. Jesus compared it to the sowing of seeds (Matthew 13:20-22). Some receive the word with joy, but cannot endure because as soon as trouble arises, the word is forsaken. Still, others receive the word, but also forsake it when they become occupied by the concerns of the world and what it has to offer. The rich young ruler is an example: he wanted eternal life, but the cost of his riches was too great (Matthew 19:16-22).

Sometimes people will not take hold of the promises of God because of unbelief, because they find it difficult or impossible to believe He will deliver what He has promised. The Israelites had such difficulty. God had promised them the land. Spies had returned and reported the land as indeed all God said it would be (Numbers 13:27). But some also described the people of the land as strong giants living in fortified cities (vs. 28). Based on the account of the skeptical spies, the Israelites wept, complained, lamented their predicament and situation, and they began to make plans to return to Egypt (Deuteronomy 14:1-4). They did not believe God would do what He said.

One problem was that Israel was relying on **her** strength: "… and we were like grasshoppers in our own sight, and so we were in their sight" (Deuteronomy 13: 33). They were not looking at the power of God. When we rely on our abilities, we have taken our eyes from the might and proficiencies of God. We are counting on our capacity to achieve the goals. It is at this point we have entered into the zone of probable inadequacy. We are not able to accomplish on our own, even when we think we are. The ignorance resulting from our pride and arrogance causes us to believe we have brought successful results to fulfillment through our personal efforts. Scripture plainly informs that without Christ, we can do nothing (John 15:5b). Using human abilities may result in a modicum of progress, but true success and long lasting fruitfulness can only come from God.

When God says to possess "the land," we can know He has already paved the way and provided all that will be needed to take control of it, to be successful. "Behold, I am driving out from before you the Amorite and the Canaanite and the Hittite and the Perizzite and the Hivite and the Jebusite" (Exodus 34:11). "No man shall be able to stand against you; the Lord your God will put the dread of you and the fear of you upon all the land where you tread, just as he said to you" (Deuteronomy 11:25). Even if we have some degree of unbelief, we can place it before the Lord and know He will provide the faith needed to possess the promise (Mark 9:17-27).

Possessing the land then is a matter of believing God, believing what He said, believing He will bring it to pass, and knowing He has already paved the way and provided all which is necessary to take hold of it. "Faith is the substance of things hoped for, the evidence of things not seen" (Hebrews 11:1). *Vine's Expository Dictionary* (1997) defines faith as "a firm persuasion, a conviction based upon hearing." "Substance," as used in this scripture, is defined as "confidence which leads one to stand under, endure, or undertake anything." The term "evidence" is denoted as "proof". What we are to do then, based on these definitions, is upon hearing the promises of God, to be firmly persuaded and convinced that we have what we have hoped for, although it may not be visible to the physical eye at this time. We are to have the confidence that causes us to stand and endure anything because we have the proof that He will deliver what He has promised. Our proof lies in the fact that our God cannot lie (Titus 1:2) and whatever He purposes shall come to pass (Numbers 23:19). No emissaries from the enemy can deter us, whether they are our circumstances, feelings, or doubtful whisperings, because we know we are assured of the victory. "Now thanks be to God Who **always** (emphasis added) leads us in triumph in Christ, and through us diffuses the fragrance of His knowledge in every place" (2nd Corinthians 2:14). Therefore we must determine in our hearts, even before doubt arises, that we will stand until the promise is manifested. As evidence of our faith, we will do the victory march, that is, worship, praise, and give thanks even before the "battle" is over because we know it has already been won.

XVII.

Remembering the Victory and Standing in the Triumph

The children of Israel were preparing to cross over into the Promised Land. Moses had died and the Lord had established Joshua as their leader (Joshua1:1-10). After they crossed the Jordan, the Lord commanded Joshua to have twelve appointed men to each take a stone from the midst of the Jordon, and after crossing, set them up in the place where they would lodge for the night (4:1-3). He instructed that these stones would be a memorial for their children to explain the miracle of the dried up waters of the Jordan (vs. 21-24). By the stones, the people of the earth would also know the Lord is mighty and is to be feared forever.

Michael and Melissa now have the ministry God promised. It was a journey filled with mountains and valleys, and much of the road led them through the wilderness. Although they are excited about being in this new place, they are also apprehensive about the future paths. How will they be able to stand?

Receiving the crown and participating in the march of victory feels very good. Emotions are high, and all the world appears to be applauding. What could possibly go wrong from here? Most, if not all of us, once we reach the "promised land," would like to think our troubles are over, at least the major ones. However, that is almost never the case. "Many are the afflictions of the righteous, but the Lord delivers him out of them all" (Psalm 34:19). To name a few possible afflictions: the present occupants of the land do not want to surrender what now belongs to you; the people you thought were with you begin to take on the ways of the old occupants; someone in your camp does something that God has explicitly instructed not to do, and because of his/her rebellion and disobedience, the flow of the blessings are hindered; those in your camp rebuild their old idols and begin to worship them; the people who have pledged themselves to God now desire and assume another god which they allow to have rule over them; or they began to so intermingle with the old occupants of the land, they are hardly recognizable as people of God. We find we need God as much, or even more, than before we entered into our promise.

The scripture warns that we are vulnerable when we have entered into the promises:

Beware that you do not forget the Lord your God by not keeping His commandments, His judgments, and His statutes which I command you today, lest—when you have eaten and are full, and have built beautiful houses and dwell in them; and when your herds and your flocks multiply, and your silver and your gold are multiplied, and all that you have is multiplied; when your heart is lifted up, and you forget the Lord your God who brought you out of the land of Egypt, from the house of bondage; who led you through the great and terrible wilderness, in which were fiery serpents and scorpions and thirsty land where there was no water; who bought water for you out of the flinty rock; who fed you in the wilderness with manna, which your fathers did not know, that He might humble you and that He might test you, to do you good in the end—then you say in your heart, "My power and the might of my hand have gained me this wealth" (Deuteronomy 8:11-17).

Therefore living in the victory of the promise can cause us to forget what God has done and cause us to think it was by our competence and effort that these things have been accomplished. If this becomes our thinking pattern we will also begin to believe that the responsibility for maintaining the possession lies solely on us. That's why the Israelites were directed by God to take memorial stones. It is also the reason we must gather them, so during the times of forgetfulness, we can go back to our stones and remember what the Lord has done, that it was He Who brought it to pass. We can also explain to our children, while reminding ourselves, what the stones mean. For example, one stone might mark the time when you had no food and God provided your "manna." Another stone may indicate the times when you were ill and He held up the "bronze serpent" (Numbers 21:9) in your wilderness, and you were healed. You might recall that another stone was placed when you had little, if any money and He did not allow your "garments or sandals to wear out." Still another stone might remind of the time when He caused the "fear of you to come upon your enemies," when He "subdued" them so that you might cross over and possess the promise. These will have to be the things that sustain us during the turbulent times. They will remind us of the faithfulness of God. We will remember He can be trusted. The stones will bring to our minds the fact that we have nothing to fear or dread. He will not allow us to be overtaken by the situation or our circumstances. They will whisper to us that no matter what things appear to be, we can rely on the word of God. These rocks will remind us that He has already gone before us and prepared the way just as He did with the Israelites (Joshua 3:3). These memorials will help us keep in mind that God fights for us (Deuteronomy 1:30; 2nd Chronicles 16:9). They will awaken within us the memory of Him standing between us and our enemies (Exodus 14:19). The stones will be a reminder that all things will work together for our good. In retrospect, we will recall that He has never failed us, that whatever He has purposed in our lives shall come to pass: "Commit your way to the Lord, trust also in Him, and He shall bring it to pass" (Psalm 37:5). These many stones of remembrance will strengthen our faith and help us to stand regardless of the boisterous winds and treacherous waves. We will then be able to declare that our light affliction is but for a moment (2nd Corinthians 4:17). We will be comforted because we will not look at the things which are seen, but at the things which are not seen. It will sustain us to know that these things are working for our benefit, for our growth and character development, and that they are preparing us for our destination. Our confidence will not be cast away because we are assured that in a short while He Who is coming will come (Hebrews 10:35, 37). This season cannot last forever. It has a definite time span. Because He has declared our destiny, it must come to pass. Our lives are ones of continuous mountain and valley experiences, but we have the confidence that whatever the situation, the Lord is with us and it will work for our good. We are always victorious.

XVIII.

Conclusion

The Israelites provide a vivid portrait of a wilderness journey. The Exodus account reveals what was to become their patterned relationship with God. We read of their enslavement and how God heard their cries and designated Moses as the one who would lead them out of Egypt. When Moses informed them of the prophecy, they worshipped, however, they had not counted on things getting worse before they would get better. In the midst of the pre-deliverance tribulations, they became hard hearted, but after the miracles when they left Egypt with plunder, they rejoiced and were joyful. Then came the obstacle of the Red Sea. Confronted with the sea in front of them and Pharaoh behind them, they first responded by praying, but afterward, very quickly, they yielded to complaining and bitterness. After the Red Sea miracle, the Israelites sang songs of praise, but shortly after the songs came complaints about the insufficiency of water. Soon thereafter, they complained about the food, after which they complained about water again. Later they would recommit to the Lord, however while Moses was on the mountain receiving the Ten Commandments, they were below making a golden calf idol.

This was the pattern of the Israelites. They continuously had trouble believing God. Even when they were told to take the land which **God** had given them, they did not believe He was able to deliver what He said He would.

What then can be learned from their experiences and related to our own? Deuteronomy 8 teaches us several things:

- The wilderness is a place to humble you, to test you and to know what is in your heart (vs. 2). Will you continue to obey God no matter what the circumstances? Will you trust Him with your life? During the testing, will you acknowledge and allow your heart to be ruled by His sovereignty? Will you allow Him to totally control everything that concerns you? Will you pledge your allegiance to Him simply because He is? Will you acknowledge that he does indeed have a right to do what He determines with those things which are His?

- In the wilderness God will show you a new thing (vs. 3). He will give you "manna" which neither you nor "your fathers" have known before. Many times the wilderness will place you in a position which you have not previously experienced. This situation will call for you to learn and encounter God in a new way. Whereas in the past you may have relied on your own resources to take care of and sustain you, those things will not be at your disposal now, or they will be insufficient for your needs. He will be your only provider and through the experience, perhaps for the first time, you will come to know Him as Jehovah-jireh (God Our Provider) and El Shaddai (All-Sufficient God).

- God will sustain you in a way you did not think possible – in a supernatural way (vs. 4). You will find that although you have no personal provisions, neither your "garments nor your sandals will wear out" and your "feet will not swell." Often times you will find that, although you have not been able to contribute to your sustenance, you have not lacked anything you really needed. You have no explanation other than the care and power of God. You now have a testimony that is truly your own and one which will sustain you when other turbulent times arise.
- The wilderness is a time of discipline designed to make you more like Christ (vs.

5). It is a time to develop character, character which will carry you and keep you in the places God has ordained you to be. At the time Joseph received the dream revealing his future prominence, he was not ready to assume the position. He needed to develop wisdom, the kind of wisdom that teaches there is a time to share dreams. When those who currently have dominion and authority over you are already feeling hostile toward you, this is not a good time to tell them that the fulfillment of your revelation will bring them under submission to you. Joseph had to learn that the dreams which are from God must be released in His way and His time. Their fulfillment is to further His purposes and therefore they must be orchestrated by Him. Although David was King as soon as Samuel by the direction of God anointed Him, he could not assume the throne until he had learned how to function in the court, how to deal with situations he had not created and ones over which he had no control, and how to persevere under the most hostile of circumstances. All of us must be groomed to assume the places God has established for us.

- The wilderness is designed to teach us reverence for God, Godly fear, and to teach us Who is in control (vs. 6). In this place we are vulnerable. There are wild beasts and many other dangers lurking in places which are hidden from our view. We do know if God does not lead us, we can be consumed by any one of those threats. We know if He stands back and leaves us to our own devices, we will not make it out of that area unharmed. We know we have not passed this way before. We are in new territory and on new terrain; we are not familiar with either. If we are to survive and come out unharmed, God will have to direct the way and protect us on the journey. Rebellion, stubbornness, deceit, independence, or pride can not be afforded. The presence of these indicates that we are trusting in our own ability and have a desire to do it on our own, our own way. However, once either of the above surfaces, we become very aware that we do not know the environment, and unless we submit to the hand of God, we will perish. It is at this juncture we truly learn we are not our own and without Him we can do nothing.

- In this place you are being prepared for the promise, being relieved of the things which will be hindrances to you in the new place (vs. 7). New wine calls for new wineskins. Sometimes we believe we are ready to "possess the land", but vestiges of "Egypt" remain within us. In the crevices of our minds, we may be holding on to the false gods of the peoples of the old land (like faith in our own abilities). Moreover, some of the people may even be traveling with us. If they have chosen to accompany us, we must know how to walk with them while not allowing them to contaminate us. Also, memories from the past that hinder our future progress must be discarded. Looking back to perceived better times when challenges arise invites a temptation to turn back or creates the atmosphere for grumbling and complaining. To do either would displease God and could result in forfeiting the prize. In either case, the loss is ours. Scripture points out that "No one having put his hand to the plow, and looking back, is fit for the kingdom of God" (Luke 9:62). Additionally, the wilderness provides the opportunity for the enemies of success to be removed, enemies such as pride, unforgiveness, unrepentant sin, rebellion, self-centeredness, a haughty spirit and the like. These are characteristics that will sabotage your progress and bring your success to a premature ending. The wilderness will provide you with those things needed to keep you in the place of exaltation. If you will allow, it will humble you. "For whoever exalts himself will be humbled, and he who humbles himself will be exalted" (14:11).

- The wilderness can give you a new appetite (Deuteronomy 8:8). The children of Israel tired of the manna God had provided (Numbers 11:5-6) and yielded to the yearnings and appetites of the past. They craved the food of Egypt that they now remembered so vividly. It may be they did not eat to the degree they imagined. Things in retrospect are frequently remembered with more favor and embellishment than they were in reality. Even if their memories matched the actual situation, there is no comparison between the two situations because nothing can truly surpass what God provides. The food of Egypt was not equal to the food from the very hand of God. The truth is that the change which became necessary because of God's extraordinary provision challenged the ordinary, fleshly nature to which the Israelites had become accustomed. To take hold of and occupy the "promised land" requires a change in our appetites. Our tastes must be ones which can only be appeased by the things of God, our hunger and thirst being satisfied solely by Him. To truly ensure success we will have to want only what He wants for us, and only want to acquire it in the way He ordains. True fulfillment lies in being satisfied with what He provides and submitting to the way He provides it.

- You can be prepared for more prosperous work in this deserted place (Deuteronomy 8:9). Your survival in the wilderness may depend on you developing creativity and gaining knowledge and skills. These very things will increase your ability to make use of what the promised place requires and offers. In the wilderness you can learn how to endure when few resources are available or how to make the most of the resources you have. For example, in the wilderness, the Israelites surely would have had to learn to use what was around them to make tools and implements needed for their day-to-day tasks and for protection and battle. In your wilderness, you may have learned to make scarce resources last longer and go further. You may have learned to take what was around you and make it into food, food you never had before or even knew existed. The promised place may initially have few resources. In the wilderness, you will have learned how to maximize them. Moreover, in the new place, you may not have the assistance you need. The wilderness can provide the opportunity to learn how to depend on God alone to bring your goals to successful completion. Learning to allow Him to work through you will surely be one of the most advantageous byproducts of the wilderness. It can show you that if you allow Him to give you the will and the ability for the tasks, you will accomplish your goals.

- Testimonies are established as a result of the wilderness experience (Deuteronomy 8:10). *Vine's Expository Dictionary* (1997) defines a testimony "as witness and evidence." *Webster's Dictionary* (1983) expands on the idea by explaining it as "firsthand authentication of a fact." If the wilderness has done its perfect work in us, based on our personal experience, we will be able to proclaim as fact the things which God has declared about Himself. We will be able to attest that He is the Most High, the Lord God Almighty Who is first and foremost holy. We will also attest to the fact that He is a great God Who is all sufficient and faithful. We will know that no matter where we are, He is the God Who sees. It is not unlikely that we will have come to know Him as our Banner, Healer, Host, and Peace. We will have discovered the joy of knowing that He is the One Who sanctifies. Because we have come to this knowledge, we will eagerly and delightfully share it with others. It will be our desire for them to learn the Lord as He has revealed Himself to us. We will want others to have the assurance that all they could ever need or wish for lies within His power to provide and grant.

- Essential to our wilderness survival is continual praise. To praise is "to express a favorable judgment of" (Merriam-Webster, 1983). It is to commend or "recommend as worthy of confidence." Having obtained the provisions in the wilderness, having been delivered from danger, and having been given the stamina to be steadfast are just a few of the reasons to praise God and to declare Him as trustworthy. Praise is a joyous sound in the ears of God because it shows Him our commitment and our view of Him as praiseworthy, in spite of the circumstances. It shows we love and appreciate Him above anyone and everything. Heavy hearts and downcast spirits cannot remain where sincere praise is resounded. Praise causes one to focus on the One being praised, and when the focus is shifted to Him, peace and a sense of security will result. Scripture tells us the Lord will keep the person whose mind is stayed on Him in perfect peace, not just because his mind is on Him, but because that person trusts God (Isaiah 26:3). Darkness must flee when the overshadowed place is illuminated by the Light. The gloomy, uninhabited, uncultivated place will shine, increase, and foster growth when the Source of joy, comfort, and the Tiller of the ground is acknowledged for Whom He is and all He does.

- Perhaps the most valuable lesson to be learned in the wilderness, and surely one of the most liberating, is realizing that God is sovereign and it is He Who controls our lives (Deuteronomy 8:14-20). Knowing He reigns supreme and that He will guide and direct us if we allow Him, can set us free from the perceived need to be in charge, from the feeling that the events of our life must be controlled by us in order to assure the desired outcome. Knowing our view is partial and God's is complete can cause us to relax in His wisdom and care. The internal knowledge that He makes all things work together for our good decreases worry and provides us the freedom to rest in His will. We can face everyday with one, and only one, concern: pleasing God. That alone reduces our list of cares to the single focus of being led by the Spirit of God. His Spirit resides in us to teach us and lead us in all things (John 14:26; Romans 8:14). Our only responsibility is to listen and obey.

What then do you do while in the wilderness?

1. **Do not try to escape it.**
2. **Listen for God.**
3. **Stay in close, intimate communication with Him through prayer, praise, worship, and His word.**
4. **Obey Him.**

5. Allow Him to remove all idols and obstacles that obstruct your way and hinder your possession of the "promised land."
6. Observe what God is doing and build memorial stones as reminders of His works.
7. Use discernment concerning those whom you allow to accompany you during your sojourn in the wilderness and those from whom you receive assistance while there.
8. Submit under the mighty hand of God and surrender all that you are and hope to be, your desires, your expectations, and everything that concerns you. Allow Him to

make you new wine and give you a new wineskin. Become a new creation.

9. Above all, you will want to keep your eyes on Christ. Focusing on Him will prevent you from being overtaken by your surroundings. Peter walked on the water as long as he looked at Christ, but the moment he moved his eyes, shifted his focus, he began to drown (Matthew 14:28-31). Do not permit that to happen to you.

Behold, I will do a new thing,

Now it shall spring forth;

Shall you not know it?

I will even make a road in the wilderness

And rivers in the desert (Isaiah 43:19).

References

MacArthur, J. (1997). The MacArthur Study Bible. New King James Version. Nashville, TN: Thomas Nelson.

Merriam-Webster, A. (1983). Webster's ninth new collegiate dictionary. Springfield, MA: Merriam-Webster, INC.

Vine, W.E. (1997). Vine's expository dictionary. Nashville, TN: Thomas Nelson.

Youngblood, R.F. (1995). New illustrated Bible dictionary. Nashville, TN: Thomas Nelson.